For Lara.

May your Saturday shifts always be covered.

polari plays

Published by Polari Plays, an imprint of Polari Press.

polari.com @polaripress

ISBN: 978-1-914237-15-7

First published in the UK in 2023.

Cover design and typesetting by Peter Collins for Polari. Typeset in a custom typeface by Bijou Type and Roslindale by David Jonathan Ross. Cover photograph by Kate Bones. Printed on responsibly sourced paper using vegetable inks. Polari Press is committed to reducing its environmental impact.

A catalogue record for this book is available from the British Library.

To find out more about our authors and work, visit polari.press and sign up to our newsletter.

louis rembges

chatham house rules

Presented by The Goat Exchange.

First performed at Pleasance Courtyard, Bunker One, Edinburgh Fringe on Wednesday, 2 August 2023.

Written & performed by Louis Rembges
Director Mitchell Polonsky
Producer Ellen Larson
Stage Manager Abigail Sage
Set Designer Ella Lynch
Lighting Designer Finn Bamber

cast & creative team

LOUIS REMBGES

Writer and Performer

Louis is a Sheffield-born writer and actor living in London. His work has been performed at The Pleasance, VAULTS, Brixton Jamm, Brixton Base, Mountview, the Bunker Theatre and Museum of the Home. He is a member of The Goat Exchange theatre company, performing with them in the UK and internationally. He is an alumnus of the Royal Court's Intro to Playwriting Group and recipient of the BOLD 2023 Playwriting Prize. Recent credits include: *Cat on a Hot Tin Roof* (Provincetown Tennessee Williams Festival); and *Jason* (VAULTS Festival). As a writer: *It's Raining on Prom Night* (BOLD Studios); *On Railton Road* (Museum of the Home); and *Facehugger* (Mountview).

MITCHELL POLONSKY

Director

Mitchell is the co-artistic director of The Goat Exchange, with whom he has directed more than twenty productions including: *Deadclass Ohio* (Ice Factory Festival); *Jason* (VAULT Festival); *Memonica* (HERE Arts Center); *7 Blowjobs* (La Mama); *Cat on a Hot Tin Roof* and *Sex* (Provincetown Tennessee Williams Festival); *Two Character Play* and *Titanic*

Plays (The Bunker); *The Emperor's New Clothes* (A.R.T.); *Antigone* (Harvard Stadium); *[Othello] Desdemona* (Sanders Theatre); *Streetcar [I Don't Want Realism]* (Farkas Hall); and *Salome, or the Cult of the Clitoris: A Historical Phallusy* (The Lir). He has also worked as an associate director with Tania Bruguera, Daniel Kramer, and Sam Gold. Mitchell studied Theatre, Dance and Media at Harvard College and was awarded a George J. Mitchell fellowship to pursue an MFA in Theatre Directing from Trinity College in Dublin.

ELLEN LARSON

Producer

Ellen is a freelance theatre producer, facilitator and theatremaker. Producing credits include, as trainee producer for Paines Plough: *Hungry*; *Really Big and Really Loud*; *May Queen*; *Black Love* (Roundabout 2021 tour); *Reasons You Should(n't) Love Me* (Kiln, 2021). As assistant producer for Paines Plough: *Sorry, You're Not a Winner* (regional tour 2022); *Sessions* (regional tour 2021); *A Sudden Violent Burst of Rain*; *Half-Empty Glasses*; *The Ultimate Pickle!* (Roundabout 2022 tour and Edinburgh Fringe Festival); *Reasons You Should(n't) Love Me* (regional tour 2022). As creative producer for Moon House Theatre: *The Neat Freak* (Buxton Fringe 2019 and regional tour 2021); *The Twelve Days of Goblin-Mas* (online short film, 2020); *The Homeless Guide to a Hand Up* (Chapel Playhouse, London, 2019);

and *Get Your Greek On!* (online video series, 2021). She is associate organiser (access) for BAP! Ellen has an MA in Theatre for Community and Education at Mountview.

ABIGAIL SAGE

Stage Manager

Abigail has worked with The Goat Exchange since 2018 on projects including: *The Emperor's New Clothes* (American Repertory Theatre); *Memonica* (HERE Arts Center);, *Cat on a Hot Tin Roof* (Provincetown Tennessee Williams Festival); and *Jason* (VAULT Festival). She is a lighting designer and stage manager based in London.

ELLA LYNCH

Set Designer

Ella is an artist from Watford who works primarily in sculpture, collage and costume. She experiments with scale and incorporates found objects, drawing inspiration from the British high street and pop iconography. The V&A featured one of Lynch's costumes as the final piece in *Fashioning Masculinities: The Art of Menswear* exhibition (London, 2022). Lynch's work has been recognised by the British Fashion Council and has been acknowledged in publications such as British and Italian *Vogue*, *ID* and *Dazed & Confused*.

FINN BAMBER

Lighting Designer

Finn is a Boston-based lighting designer and photographer. His work spans dance, plays, musicals, opera, concerts, site specific/immersive performance and virtual performance across more than fifty productions. For The Goat Exchange: *Deadclass Ohio* and *Jason* (VAULTS Festival); *Cat on a Hot Tin Roof* (Provincetown Tennessee Williams Festival); *Memonica* (HERE Arts Center); and *Streetcar [I Don't Want Realism]* (Farkas Hall). Other recent credits include: *House of Ramon Iglesia*; *Torch Song*; and *Marriage or Maid/MADE*.

acknowledgements

Chatham House Rules began life as a pitch to director (and legend) Emily Aboud and producer (and legend) Grace Dickson, who produced the early version of the show in 2022.

The stunning team of Mitchell Polonsky, Ellen Larson, Abbie Sage and The Goat Exchange then took on the play for a run at the Edinburgh Fringe in 2023 at The Pleasance, and thanks to their support (and Ella Lynch's giant pair of David Cameron legs) the play became the version printed here.

Note: This version of the script went to print before the first completed run of the production, and future performances may differ slightly from what is written here.

Chatham House Rules

by Louis Rembges

A one-person play

HOST *late twenties, male identifying.*

Other characters (played by HOST*):*

LARGEFOREHEAD MAYBEFACELIFT

AGGRESSIVELY ORGANISED

NOTHINGBEHIND THEEYES

MEAGAIN

FRAZZLED BOGGLER

EATSBANANA FAST

RUINME PLEASE

PIGFUCKER

FLORENCE PUGH

HER

LOOKSLIKE APAUL

Notes on the text

All parts to be played by one performer. Capitalisation and structure is to help the actor with delivery but can be ignored.

A full stop (.) denotes a beat or a pause.

A comma (,) at the end of a character's dialogue denotes an interruption. An em-dash (—) denotes a character interrupting themselves.

Italicised lines are to other characters, not to the audience.

Words in parentheses () are an aside, words in square brackets [] don't have to be spoken.

Anything marked with an asterisk (*) or in a rounded box *should be projected, but this can also be ignored.*

The TikTok content in the play should be updated to whatever is trending at the time/relatable to the individual performer.

In this production **PIGFUCKER** *is represented by an inanimate pair of legs.*

Hello

0

A jetpack taking off. Or is it a message sending?

HOST *desperately needs to leave.*

HOST MEDIUM VENTI CASHEW MILK FLAT WHITE
SORRY WE CAN'T DO GOAT'S CHEESE WE HAVEN'T
GOT ANY FRIDGES
What?
Sorry. Don't know what happened there. Little brain fart. Let me start again.

0.5

HOST *desperately needs to leave. Every character on the call is dressed in hospital scrubs, but no one references it*

HOST Welcome to the Myopic Technology Showcase 2023
now if I could just Squeeze through here,
Toilet? Right behind you,
Well Venti means Large so you can have a venti Or a medium,
Toilet? Right behind you,
Sorry we can't do goat's cheese we don't have the right fridges,

Toilet? Just close your eyes run at the wall and believe,
Cashew milk? Wonderful choice,
No sir the wine's not corked it's got a cork In it so it
needs Opening I'll be right with you.
Can you just, excuse me, no
EVERYBODY PLEASE. CAN YOU ALL FUCK OFF I'M
KILLING SOMEONE ON TIKTOK AND I'M MISSING
THE BEST BITS.

SZA, Doja Cat 'Ding'.

Kidding.

Blackout.

Prologue

Everything that happens in this universe is real.

HOST *(in the dark)* Hello.

That didn't really happen. Me saying that last thing.

That would have been really dumb.

I just sort of made a smiley excuse, dragged you in here by the legs and closed the door.

It's broken, the door, you can't open it from the outside the handle's fallen off. Doesn't matter.

If I had told someone, or if someone had seen, we wouldn't be here. It wouldn't be now.

I hope you can still hear me.

I don't know how best to tell you.

A light from his phone.

I've actually got everything in here. In my drafts. On TikTok.

I'll play them all for you!

Structure them in like a fun narrative loop. A visual story.

A pitch, before we go live.

A presentation. A Compilation.

(A la Tik Tok influencer) So. Storytime.

1

A highway and an auditorium.

HOST The Prologue, if we were to have a prologue, would be something like this:
It's an idea. A great idea.
Feeling. Viral.

Highway.

HOST OK babes, this is it. Me and you. Thank you so much for doing this by the way I love you I promise I'll cover your Saturday. I've got a good feeling about this. This is the one,

Auditorium.

LARGEFOREHEAD Welcome. If you don't know who I am; where have you been? Aha, my name is Largeforehead Maybefacelift, co-founder and executive chairman of Myopic and 8ball Capital, £240m seed fund with a global remit and over 100 unicorn founders. Now,

Highway.

HOST The idea is, it's a really good one, make sure you get the whole road in behind me yeah cos I wanna really get the feeling of,

Auditorium.

LARGEFOREHEAD Pride. Previously I co-founded longarm.com in 1998 and then sold it to Acre, for 1.1bn. Then, Turbo PowHER: European network taking action to change the underrepresentation of women in AI development. And most recently, Build An Heir: The world's first on demand AI development school, and yet, standing here in front of you all right now.
I am the least successful person in the room.

Long round of applause.

Now, I think you're all ready for a bit of,

Highway.

HOST ACTION! OK, so just like the Tories back-pedalled from Boris to Liz and back to Boris this week over a LETTUCE, I'm gonna pedal this Bike, Backwards, over a dual carriageway. How about that,

Auditorium.

LARGEFOREHEAD For an amazing few days, huh?
Now allow me to introduce our final speaker of this year's Myopic colloquy. Who navigated the country's practically teleological shift in 2016's political landscape, for better or for worse, using deft sleight of

hand and masterful curation of flare-gun-suicide press exposés—Oink Oink—

Laughter.

Now please put your hands together for,

Highway.

HOST Fucks sake do we have to do it again? Are we live? Oh god sorry my fault OK let's go and watch out for that railing you'll smack your head and kill yourself.
OK TAKE TWO,

A smack and BLACKOUT.

A crescendo of social media tweets, pings, feed refreshes, WhatsApp dings, TikTok clips: automated voice 'my chonky boi can't use the stairs', Cardi B VO 'I don't even have time for my love life, to see my family, I don't have time for nothing, I'm working every single day, I'm depressed!', 'PICKPOCKET!!', Ceilings by Lizzie McAlpine, Bombastic Side Eye, 'Two bros! Sitting in a hot tub!', 'Oh no, our table, it's broken', etc. etc. building into Kiss Me More by Doja Cat & SZA, the 'Ding' reverberating round the space.

2

SCREEN RECORD. WhatsApp. **HOST** *sits on stage and reads aloud Aggressively Organised's voice notes, and types his own messages into the chat.*

HOST *(typing)* Hello?

Really sorry for the late response.

Is this still up for grabs?

Thanks for thinking of me.

Host

x

A voice note from **AGGRESSIVELY** *comes through.*

He plays it.

AGGRESSIVELY (VN) Host!! Ohmygod.

It's so nice to talk to you!

How have you been!

How is everything!

What have you been up to!

HOST Hello,

Yeah I'm good thanks yeah

Sorry I didn't reply sooner I've actually been off social media lol.

I've been recording everything though for this thing.

A very long voice note.

AGGRESSIVELY So I'm in all this, I don't wanna say recruitment, my bosses don't call it recruitment but it's Basically recruitment.
So it's like a well it Is a high profile networking event for like tech, and business politicians.
There are usually Crazy over the top guests like Thefrogwho Madefacebook, Crunchyeyes Microsoft, all of Dragons Den, Monarchy Shouldntbetradingwiththem and Newlabour Shouldbeinjail,

HOST omg.

AGGRESSIVELY Ohmygod and last year Nicevoice Tortoiseface came! He's so cute and old and nice and did a talk on like, the planet.

HOST omg.

AGGRESSIVELY Yeah about the polar bears floating all the way down to the Galapagos because their ice houses had fallen down or something. So sad.
And Spiderlady Judge came to the first ever one! Bless her RIP!
This is my first sort of managing for them, event wise, It's gonna be a super special one.
Everyone has to be called by their first name. Everyone's equal, no one has a title.
So Dianasbalding Son would just be Dianasbalding.
It's like a day of really amazing talks and discussions and tech demonstrations like Making A Billion Dollar

Business Even Bigger.

And climate.

It's super inspiring even to just Observe people, you know?

Exciting!

And it's all at the Stunning Animal Farmhouse in the Cotswolds—you'll be at a cute hotel nearby!

HOST omg.

AGGRESSIVELY Also it's run under Chatham House Rules.

Super important.

So no one can share details of what's being heard or seen.

Completely confidential, so no naming names!

You'll need to fill out the online reference form so just cite me, Aggressively Organised, as your referee, OK?

HOST omg. OK, I'm in.

AGGRESSIVELY Thank you Host.

There's no press and all social media is strictly controlled and limited to the Myopic team.

So no TikTokking on site babes OK?

Haha!

Anyway, amazing, so glad to have you on board.

I'll see at the Zoom training on Friday.

Exciting!

3

SCREEN RECORD. Zoom. It's connecting. In this version of the play, the other participants are all played and pre-recorded by **HOST** *and projected onto a screen while* **HOST** *sits downstage and joins in on his phone. Whenever* **HOST** *speaks, the Zoom training should still be ongoing behind him.*

AGGRESSIVELY Exciting!
Welcome to the Zoom training folks, we're just gonna give it a few more minutes...

HOST Test mic? No thank you.
Mute. Forever.

NOTHINGBEHIND THEEYES Let me just start by saying how happy I am to have you all here. Virtually. Which is fitting. Aha. My name is Nothing Behindtheyes, I'm the lead event CSM for Myopic,
It's my ship. Ahoy.
A vessel I'm really excited to have you all aboard.
This year's event is a really exciting one. It's a game changer.
So listen closely. Your Really Important Front-Of-House Rules Are...

HOST Me on Zoom. Always the same. Just staring at myself.
Just staring at myself.
(A la Keira Knightley) 'I look quite pretty.'

NOTHING Everybody will have been screened and given a pass. Check the name badges. Discreetly.

They will either be moss green, or sage green.

During this **EATSBANANA FAST** *appears on screen because she forgot to turn her mic off. She noisily eats a banana in two impressive bites. She notices, panics and closes her laptop.* **NOTHING***'s speech continues, unaware.*

NOTHING There are six stages throughout the event site, please refer to the map in your emails, and to the set list. We're a bit like Glastonbury. Your favourites will probably clash. Aha.

Any questions?

HOST Typing pictures of dumb bitch into Google.

(As Keira) 'They're all of me!'

NOTHING Five hundred guests, in response to your question, Meagain.

You are expected to be on comms at all times.

If you see this—highly unlikely I must say—

Politely ask guests to delete any photos they have taken...

HOST 'I'm nice. I really am. Apart from my terrible taste in pie.' This is Keira Knightley if you hadn't realised. 'I've just tried the wedding video and it's a complete disaster, it's come out all blue and wibbly.' 'No I won't tell them it's carol singers you horrible little man.' 'Johnny was a nightmare on *Pirates*,'

AGGRESSIVELY Host?

HOST Yes. Yes? Hello.

NOTHING Something you wanted to add?

HOST What? Shit No God sorry I thought I was on mute, I was just doing [Keira Knightley],

NOTHING Please pay attention.

MEAGAIN Me again! I just wanted to ask for a couple of examples of tasks we'll be asked to perform on the day?

AGGRESSIVELY Ooh I can take this one! So for instance you'll be asked to have gloves on when you make sure the guests have their ear plugs ready to use at 16.30 because of the jetpack demonstration at 17.00.
It's really important you get this right because it will literally be two jets flying in close proximity to the dining tables.

.

NOTHING It was so exciting talking with you all, I'm confident we're in the best hands to usher us through the day. I've got to shoot off now, but before I do, we've been notified of a little security breach.
Someone has replaced one of our guests on the list.
A journalist most likely,
Not an assassin. Ha ha.
But as this event is run under Chatham House Rules,
we will protect our guests' privacy until our last,
gasping breath.

You will need to go over the profiles of all the guests in the PDF pack.
I expect you all to be familiar with the list. A fun carpool activity perhaps.
Long story short, spot the person who isn't there, and tell me immediately.
And with that, I'll see you next week.
Thanks again, so much, We really can't wait to have you.

4

HOST Have you ever been in a Fiat 500 before?
It's not actually a car.
It's actually a vibrator on wheels HEYOOOOO,
Sorry. I'm nervous. Setting the scene.
I know I keep acknowledging You,
I'm sorry. It's a bit awkward.
It would be better if you could look at me.
Give me a sign.
But. So. I'll make this as visceral as possible for you.
Every necessary detail.
It's hot. It's really hot. Now, and also then. I've got a problem with time
I know I should just pick a tense.
I'm sweating. Sweaty. Now. Then.
I'm sat in the back—by the way I'm sorry about the

gaffer tape—

I'm dripping onto Frazzled Boggler's handbook next to me on the back seat.

She doesn't mind, she's laminated it.

Did you pre-empt someone sweating next to you in the car?

FRAZZLED BOGGLER *(calm)* Yes. *(Extends a hand.)* Frazzled Boggler, nice to meet you.

HOST If you hadn't noticed I've changed the names of those involved thanks to the rules, protecting myself. But to keep things fun and moving and Fun instead of picking Sophie or Imran or Charlie I've used my initiative my storytelling Prowess and captured the Essence of the person I'm talking about. Their soul. Once spoken, these names materialise the person into this space in their intended form. Their own Mothers would recognise them from these names.

EATSBANANA Pass me another one of those bananas.

HOST *Theeeeere you go Eatsbanana Fast*—some of these names are more physical.

You two didn't actually try to memorise the entire guestlist? Five hundred people?

EATSBANANA We're just freelance goblins with no lives or singular thoughts outside the job in hand babe.

FRAZZLED I'm not going to be the one who lets in a Journalist Assassin and ruin my chances of getting a front-of-house agency job ever again.

I've memorised B to D. I figured I and J are already going to be screened from the reception.

EATSBANANA Aren't we doing that? The reception? *(Motions for banana)*

FRAZ *(gives banana)* No, Host and I are seating the welcome BBQ,

EATSBANANA *eats the banana.*

FRAZ Eatsbanana, you're on human signpost toilet pointing. I've decided to set up the group chat on Instagram because WhatsApp pings make me physically recoil.

HOST *I deleted mine.*
Well not fully deleted but like. Incognito. On the wagon.
A year ago actually. So. Can't we just use Telegram?
That's the legit one you wanna use if you wanna like,
Kidnap someone.

FRAZ Instagram's much better I've found everyone through their Facebook through their Zoom. Just get it back. For two days, it's not a big deal. No one pays attention to it anymore anyway, they're all on TikTok. Let me get it back for you.
I'll be able to mute you to the rest of the group if you're that bothered about people stalking you.
I really am very efficient, look in like the fifteen seconds I've been talking to you I've already made the group added everyone to it and set the big emoji at the top.

It's the beige mule (👠). Suitable for any occasion, people have already laughed.

.

HOST *Fine.*

FRAZ What's your handle and your mother's maiden name—OHmygod have you been recording us this Entire journey?

.

HOST I don't have the best relationship with social media.
I don't know who does really, it's like asking a puffin if it gets on with a cargo ship.
It's like.
Tossing a coin
Made out of poo
Accidentally into a stranger's mouth on the bus.
Funny. Or dark.
I used to talk a lot on here. On my phone. Instagram Live, Facebook Live, Twitter Live, Anything Live.
A lot a lot. I'd record everything, anything, every day, just in case of catching something Viral.
For my meme account. My me account. Me meme account.
But.
Never really going anywhere. Mid-tier thousands yes, but that's nothing. Not in the TikTok scheme of things.
But you being here will help a lot, Pigfucker. Audience

wise.

All I needed was you. And TikTok. TikTok's not a poo coin toss, it's a fucking poo pike bomb.

.

She was right. Everyone Is on here.

We'll make some actual TikToks first though. We'll post everything, Pigfucker.

I can call you Pigfucker, can't I?

Act I

Here Comes the Boy

5

TikTok. Audio only. @ttentionwhore's first post.

Black.

(Sung) Here comes the boooooy.

Light flickers. Someone on the floor. Unconscious.

Hello boy. There he is.

More light onto some form, the swollen makings of a person, a glimpse of a suit, tie, leather shoes. It's grotesque.

Welcome...

PIGFUCKER *groans wetly. His breath rattles.*

Black.

6

Animal Farmhouse. The main barn. Host and the rest of the team are getting debriefed before the welcome BBQ.

HOST The flowers are gorgeous.

Perfect.

The type of flowers that plunge effortlessly out their receptacles, cascading overboard. Muted pastels like chalk in a boarding school nursery.

I think it's supposed to be a barn.

Yep I'm being told it's a barn.

The flowers are fucking stunning.

.

Nothing Behindtheeyes isn't impressed with my observations.

NOTHING OK the guests will come through here, bags and coats here and then eat from the Myopic Welcome BBQ on the Oak terrace.

HOST It's not a working farm, it's a film set of a working farm. There's a chicken coop that artfully spills out through a gap in the fence onto the path and worker bees in teal farm wear roam around in teal milk floats and on teal bikes and use teal shit scoopers.

.

Hey. Excellent flowers.

FLORENCE PUGH Hmm?

HOST A Florence Pugh in the third-trimester-of-Midsommar-esque woman turns and peeks at me through armfuls of peacock feather ferns.

FLORENCE Oh sweetheart thank you. We grow them on site here in the orangery.
Dazzling aren't they.
But you'd never guess.

HOST She leans in slightly with the air of a step mum getting on side.

FLORENCE They're lilies.
Most common strain you can grow.
I call them harlequins.
Inbreed the right visual attributes together and you can dress them up however you like.

HOST She winks, and floats off after gifting me with potentially the dullest scandal known to man but I have to Battle the urge to follow her because Anything is more fun than a Debriefing—OHFUCKME—
The fittest specimen of a man I have ever seen (this far from a city) doing something Impeccably fit.

RUINME PLEASE *(kicking the wall and grunting)* Door's fucked again. There should be a handle here in this part of the wood but it's gone. Means you can only open it from the inside or, kicking it till the latch drops.

HOST *(shudders)* He's really fit. [Can you imagine waking up every day and just Being that fit? There are only realistically a handful of problems on the entire planet that wouldn't solve.]

NOTHING So the door's irrelevant right now. Go back to

the service area, you're waiting staff correct? I can see right now they're plating up the swordfish bellinis—
Try not to kick them too.

.

RUINME Right. Yeah. Cool.
Good luck without a cloakroom then pal.

HOST Ruinme Please walks off fitly as lily petals of realisation settle onto Nothing's face. I look at the wall again. Four pillars of gnarled metallic wood stretched from floor to ceiling and then, There.
The faintest of gaps for hinges and the hairline crack sawn into the logs where you can Just about make out the shape of a door.
Nothing Behindtheeyes I must say, the dedication to style over substance in this place is actually iconic.

.

Not the most helpful thing to say in a debriefing, I know.
I know I'm a shit I can't help it,
I'm like this hybrid of a class clown and an embittered husk of someone who used to be bullied, but now has the intellectual toolkit to bully Better, but can't because I'm 'functioning in society.'

NOTHING Thank you Host, for volunteering to be our cloakroom stand for the evening.

HOST Yeah. Deserved that.

7

Animal Farmhouse. The Welcome BBQ. Host is at his makeshift cloakroom stand.

HOST A photograph is just a bunch of light hitting a plate.
I read that once. I didn't think anything when I took it other than: This Is Good. This is memeable.
Once upon a time when I was Alan Sugar of memes this would have been posted without even thinking about it.
A true self-fulfilling prophecy, a caption along the lines of '*cannibalism being alive and well on the animal farm,*' or in that vein '*looked from pig to man and man to pig,*'
But I don't do that anymore.
So it just sits in the little recently taken window on my phone as the guests retire tipsy and full to their private cabins dotted along the twilight path.
It was fun, really. The shift. The work.
I'm actually perfect for the job. I am courteous, I am friendly, I have a naturally open face and I am exceptionally charming.
I put people at ease, I am relatable—impossibly to these, the hyper rich and obliterating successful.
I make light of the lack of cloakroom, how things left exposed are technically safer;
In the light they can always be watched.
I fold Burberry trenches into sensible squares and Tetris

Birkins into neat little stacks.

Nothing Behindtheeyes glides past and even gives me an eyebrow raise of approval.

Genuine employee of the evening. I mean look at the ecosystem I've cultivated it looks like I've been fisted and puppeteered by Marie Kondo (in her prime).

I spot Frazzled Boggler grappling with her radio and think about potentially relinquishing my post for some flimsy cutoffs in the staff tent but there's a commotion suddenly behind her by the barn door.

Can you guess where we are yet? Storywise.

It's you!

PIGFUCKER I don't care who's it is, move it. My cars all need to be together, what do you think the purpose, the definition of a security detail actually is?

No no, I'm asking you a genuine question.

HOST Taller than I thought you'd be. Not that I ever really thought about it, they always managed to make you seem unobtrusive and average, the conservative boy next door. But here you are, blue faced and towering suddenly over poor Fraz—even more sad because out of everyone here she's the only one I would have pinned to have voted for you (she's got Tory eyebrows).

PIGFUCKER I don't know you can move it to the bottom of the hill for all I care.

This is ridiculous I shouldn't have to be dealing with

this, who's in charge here?

HOST But there's no one here other than me, her, You and your team of thumbs in suits.

PIGFUCKER It's just a Tesla, not heavy, take the handbrake off and give it a push *(snorts)* there's a good girl.

HOST You wink and slap a fiver into Fraz's hand.

NOTHING Pigfucker! Hi! We're so pleased you've been able to join us.
Yes, no, yes, yes. No, I heard, we're actually making space on the grass just for you,
The valet staff are sorting it as we speak *(rims him)*.

HOST Nothing Behindtheeyes rims you, Pigfucker, as he ushers you onto the terrace, your thumbs in suits already positioning themselves around the perimeters.

PIGFUCKER Oh. Brilliant. Well then.

HOST You stop and turn around. You look briefly at me, but flick away.
Easy mistake, we're all dressed in the same teal tee shirts with the small proclamation that they're made out of seaweed, organic cotton and just a touch of natural peppermint.
You proffer a fleshy open palm at the end of an outstretched arm in Fraz's general direction.
There's a gruesome pause as she registers what you mean. A taught stillness.
And then it is cut, the string between you both and she

pelts forward, following the snapped invisible chord, giving you back your five pound note.

.

I don't go on a break the whole shift. I stay at my position and make sure everyone has their things back with a smile and the smile is genuine,
Because a photograph is just a bunch of light hitting a plate, and when I take it, from a perfect vantage point, my photo of You, Pigfucker, eating a slab of grilled pork momentarily with both hands,
A clear fatty liquid running down your chin,
I know that on the board, viewed from above, that this was Good.
I don't play chess enough to know why exactly, or what my move meant quite yet.
I just know that it was a fucking good one.

.

Would you mind if I sliced you a brief wedge of narrative context?

8

A Brief Wedge of Narrative Context. User comments and memes are all projected.

HOST The deletion of my Finsta. Me meme archive. Another play, a mini play, a tragedy.

@ttentionwhore, iconic handle I know, thought of it with my business partner.
My Karen Brady. (Well, I was Karen, she was Nick with great tits.)
Good reckoning of followers, great captions, a mixture of expertly selected vintage memes and vines (RIP)—
Gay person, straight friend *(knighting with sword)* homophobic jokes.*
Look at all those chickens.*
Be rootin', be tootin' and by God be shootin',
But most importantly Be Kind.*
A top* tier*, michelin* star* meme* experience*.
It worked because We worked.
The type of friend you meet working a horrific zero-hour contract job and make it not just bearable, but brilliant.
She was the type of friend who'd cover your Saturday.
No actually I'm chatting shit, the type of friend who'd
Think about covering your Saturday and go out anyway, but would Genuinely have a think about it.
The love of my life.
Shared my passwords. Boys. Found the memes.
Thought of the captions. Did the work. Filmed my lives.
Held the camera. Let me retake. Again and again and again and again.
Once I had this idea.
A great idea. Viral.

The highway.

@holly_naw_urgood **Mate you need to chillllllllllll**

HOST ACTION! OK, so just like the Tories back-pedalled from Boris to Liz and back to Boris this week over a LETTUCE, I'm gonna pedal this Bike, Backwards, over a dual carriageway.
How about that was that OK?

@cloudypoontip **is this meant to be a clever bit**

@seaborneriskhell **B can u go back to the memes. This is not what liberals want**

HOST Were you filming? Are we live?

@domforevertwink **Screen record. Iconic.**

HOST Oops fucks sake sorry. My fault,

@wraggclan **Like This To Increase Your Followers + Sex Drive**

HOST OK, lets go again,

@leonluvmx5 **This is weird**

HOST And watch out for that railing,

@chrisandbrianfrevr **I don't see why people gave Liz a hard time her hair is fine it's just a wig people wear wigs**

HOST You'll smack your head,

@mrsblue **soceal comntry dnt wrk on insta bb**

HOST And kill yourself,

@livmadagascardvd **aw i know where that is my dad lives near there <3**

HOST OK TAKE TWO,

@silent_faces **big up Little Chef**

Smack.

Back in the cloakroom.

HOST And then she turned too quickly and tripped and her ankle bent under her beige mule and her leg folded backwards and she disappeared over a two-foot railing. And I don't know if you've ever seen your best mate get taken out by a two-foot railing but it is the funniest thing in the world and thank Fuck she was still filming so we got it all on camera and then she looked right at me, beaming with the hilarity of the moment,
And her right eye unfocused and some blood rolled down her forehead and she said the funniest thing.

HER MEDIUM VENTI FLAT WHITE CASHEW MILK I'M SORRY WE CAN'T DO GOAT'S CHEESE WE HAVEN'T GOT ANY FRIDGES

HOST And looking at me like the twat I am she repeated herself,

HER MEDIUM VENTI FLAT WHITE

HOST The blood was rolling under her upper eyelid and she wasn't blinking,

HER CASHEW MILK I'M SORRY WE CAN'T DO
GOAT'S CHEESE
WE HAVEN'T GOT ANY FRIDGES

During the next monologue the house lights slowly come up, all theatricalities stop.

HOST And she said it while she stared at me and she said it when she fell again and she said it when she stared at the sky and she said it when I couldn't ring an ambulance because my phone was stuck on Instagram Live and she said it when a man pulled over and called one for me because I was screaming for help and she said it when it had been half an hour and she said it when it had been longer than an hour and she said it when we were in the ambulance and she said it when the paramedic who was so fit I asked him to ruin me as a joke when I was crying and another paramedic ate a banana in two bites and another paramedic looked like an Anime villain, rectangle glasses reflecting complete white all told me we had to sit in a four-hour queue of other ambulances in the hospital car park and she said it when her stretcher was placed in front of a bench of seats in A&E and she said it when our team of paramedics shift ended and were replaced by a new team of paramedics who said they had to wait with us for probably the duration of their entire shift until she'd been seen by a doctor instead of responding to new emergency service calls and she said it as a bleed in her brain spread unchecked from the succinct piece of grit that was lodged in her Zygomatic Arch and she said it when a frazzled paramedic tried to distract me with memes in an Instagram group chat and she said when we waited for the full duration of the new team's shift and another team replaced them and she said it when an American nurse with nothing behind the eyes gave me a blanket but I didn't want one I wasn't cold and she said it while we waited for eleven more hours and my phone was still recording and then she died.

Black.

@alex_isaac6 **Omg look. It's been live the whole time. That's like 27 hours. Can't fault Apple's new battery life. The 11 is fuckin sick**

9

Musical interlude in a Travelodge.

HOST *does an interpretive TikTok dance to 'Bohemian Rhapsody – CupcakKe Remix' to lighten the mood.*

It will eventually become clear that he's also trying to catch flying spiders in his hotel room.

The bridge of the song leads up to 'Mommaa...'

HOST DADDY *(music cuts off)*
Long legs, everywhere.
It says Travelodge on the side of the building which suggests the smell of a toaster conveyor belt at 6am and a Nespresso pod bar but this is definitely just a repurposed 1970s middle England GP on the side of a motorway service station.
The carpet is broken, the mirror doesn't reflect anything specific and the shower curtain keeps winking at me.
I excuse a particularly busy daddy and poke my head out into the corridor, meeting the eyes of Eastsbanana Fast doing exactly the same thing.

EATSBANANA It's like the fucking Shining!
I'm gonna have to call the RSPB for the flies in my room they're like albatrosses mate!
Did you see the group chat?

We're all gonna go WHSmiths to see if they're still selling booze, wanna come?

.

HOST *No.*

.

I do my best to scoop the rest of the daddies out of the air with my bare hands, and then I have to shut the window.
Immediately an elderly musk Rolo Yoghurts its way through the air and my clothes begin to stick to me.
The group chat—we're getting there sorry I keep segueing.
It's loading. I haven't been on here since my most viewed live to date.
It autofills @ttentionwhore's details.
There's a satisfying balloon of notifications, finally let go after a year of darkness.
And messages. Heart eyes, flames, Knives. And there's everyone! In Fraz's group, the beige mule, she's right.
Suitable for any occasion, and it Is funny.
Fuck, everyone's funny, they're all stunning legends.
And they've been Bitching. My people.
Eatsbanana even has a nickname for Nothingbehind Theeyes—foreskin arms—I don't know what she means by that exactly, but wow.

.

Look at that. Online again. The screen is shimmering

even. The white space filled with iridescent pixels flirting with me. I'd say it's like drugs but I don't want Euphoria types in their late twenties to groan at me, so I'll say it's like.

Food.

Then. In real time, a comment on a post one and a half years old...

@dr_hoggland **Did this gal move to TikTok? I need sweet memes in my life again b**

HOST Huh. Me too. I can do that babe.

The latest photo in my camera roll is already on my preview grid.

My photo of You.

I speak the caption aloud as I type. Like a maniac.

Like a main character,

'The creatures outside looked from pig to man, and from man to pig, and from pig to man again, but already it was impossible to say which was which.'

(A la Carrie Bradshaw) And just like that.

I'm relevant again.

10

Viral.

HOST Viral.

If there's a time for a mixture of Orwellian literature and the Tory equivalent of Ed Miliband's Sandwich Photo, it's now.

I float on high out of my room, past the Shining Twins and into the carpark.

Surely my chat friends will have seen the post by now (the inbuilt metrics tell me that although I've only got 13, 546 likes in half an hour, the post has been viewed over double that and in more than eighty-five countries.)

@zenon_hackneyph **Is that a Myopic convention?**

HOST Something catches my eye. My heart does a strange little kick, wobbling the fragile ankles of my euphoria for a split second.

EATSBANANA Host! Pull up a pew mate.

WHSmiths is still open, it's got everything you need. Everything. Weirdly, everything.

HOST I turn on a heel and walk back up the path toward the service station, almost forgetting to even acknowledge them. I'm glued to the phone, something is off, there's something alive in the photo, in the comments.

@anon_haywardbrown **yeah it fuckin is, we know where he is!!!**

HOST Something visceral, my phone feels hot and angry in my hand, the colours keep running down the screen and getting sucked back up like a vomited lung.

@bekind2023 **KILL KILL KILL**

HOST I feel weird. Strange.

Different.

I can see it in the notifications, the usual engagements being replaced by these blank accounts, anonymous faces, cartoon masks.

They pile up in my request box, one of them asking:

@grannysheila **What's next boss?**

HOST *(A la* Mean Girls, *delighted)* Was I The New Troll Bee?

I walk through the doors of WHSmith, the cool blast of stale air bringing me back down to earth slightly.

@jacob4digestive **Is that all ur gonna do? Take a picture? Way to stick it 2 the man hun**

HOST I walk past the tropical fish section and grab a Starbucks Iced Espresso and a bottle of gin.

@jariavers **omg i miss commenting on IG posts this feels so 90s <3**

HOST It's like they think I'm the Emmiline Pankhurst of Instagram.
I'm not throwing myself under a fucking Pighorse,
besides, that wouldn't Do anything,
Pighorses are notoriously Slow.

@thecrinch69 **That PIG wants me to QUEUE comin back from MALLORCA**

HOST And come on, what's doing anything to Pigfucker now actually gonna do?
Am about six years too late. We've got a calculator in power now, the most exciting thing he could do is turn upside down and say boobs.

@rozzers_custard **Doesn't have to be big bb. Just let him know he's fucked it**

HOST I see it on the necessities shelf by the lava lamps.
'Strong and stable, for the toughest jobs on planet Earth.'
I'm not gonna do anything. I'm not. But influencers do this type of thing all the time.
This is proper influencing: Promoting a brand with constructed intent without actually using the product at all.

@rmaingay_marx **Haven't you got the chance here to do something truly good?**

HOST I pay for my things and leave.

I angle the Extra Strong Gorilla Tape against my chest, just up to my collar, a tiny bit of skin, the graze of my chin, and take a knight with my queen.

I'm good at this.

Camera flash. The picture is projected, with the caption:

@ttentionwhore **wait and see** 😘🐂

Act II

Piggy Dippin'

The audio from the 'Piggy Dippin' by @missacevent on TikTok plays.

Light flickers again over the body on stage. Swollen, slumped in a corner.

'Piggy dippin! Piggy dippin at the piggy pond. Naah you went sausage swimmin in the water bowl, y'dipped dem fat lil toes in der. Chubba bun.'

Silence.

11

Back in the Fiat 500.

HOST In the Fiat with Eatsbanana Fast, Frazzled Boggler and Lookslike Apaul—he's new, but completely irrelevant— *(to* **LOOKSLIKE APAUL***) Sorry.* I didn't sleep last night, can you tell? You can't tell. *Can we stop for a coffee Please.*

EATSBANANA We're in the Costa queue babe.

HOST *Oh yeah please could I have a Cashew Milk Flat White Triple Shot,*
It's not on the menu but they'll do it.

EATSBANANA Good night then, Host?

HOST I don't tell them about my Viral Success, they obviously already know. I spent the rest of my night in my room with my new troll army. My legion.
We've made a plan.
A few Lives throughout the day, exposés, I can wear my bumbag across my chest and have my phone poking out like a car, like a dashcam.

EATSBANANA Have you seen the state of that waiter? Ruinme Please. Today I might try and get us both accidentally stuck in that cloakroom.

HOST Yesterday I might have gotten a bit territorial, but not today. Bigger fish to suck off.
Eatsbanana Fast you look just like a paramedic I met once.
Aggressively Organised meets us in the car park and gives us a generous breakfast of a Trail Bar and half a bottle of water.

AGGRESSIVELY EXCITING!!! MOOOOOORNING!!! (SMILES EVERYONE!!!!!) OK Team, so you've all got your Locations? Stay on comms, we might be switching a few of you round in case your feet get a bit sleepy!
But until then stay where we position you.
OK? Greeeeaaat.

HOST She cycles off on one of those teal bikes that seem to multiply if you look away from them, and we all position ourselves around the farm, and wait.
The sunshine hue of yesterday has faded for me and I see the event and the guests for what it is,
And who they are: A festering, fake, vapid nonsensical celebration of the maintenance of their wealth, nightmare humans hellbent on forever increasing the social divide, nothing more than a Tory Party Conference Hologram Circlejerk (my internet trolls have been waxing lyrical for me).
I'm given the vital role of Carpark Duty.

HOST *stands there and smiles and occasionally points people in the right direction. He slowly starts to get his phone out of his bumbag. The moment he does:*

AGGRESSIVELY Host?
Erm, put that away please. Yeah, no. Sorry.
That's most of the guests from the car park now yes?
Greeeaat. If you could just go up the hill, and stand there? Greeeaaat.
Thaaaanks Host, and I'll forget about the phone?
(Cackles.)

HOST She pootles off on her teal broom.
I strain and look for you. I panic that you were only there for the evening yesterday, in it for the Peacocking.

The flowers look atrocious in the sunlight.

They look fake, plastic, too symmetrical. Like someone just Googled 'Flower' and 3D-printed the loudest one, I mean they probably did.

If you'd already left, I don't know whether I'd have been devastated or relieved to be honest.

But then, You.

PIGFUCKER PPE. PPE. PPE.

That's where he went wrong, where he ballsed up from the start. You can't come back from that. If it was me it wouldn't have happened, still in 10. Far fewer bodies. I just wouldn't have fucked up that hard at the very first hurdle.

Should've known. He did that at school too. *(Snorts.)*

Hey. *(Clicks fingers.)* Loo?

HOST That feeling. Expanding again on my chest.

Pressure. Like twisting rock.

You, the horse I should be jumping in front of,

Me the radical activist of the modern generation, standing and smiling.

You asking 'where should I shit?'

And me saying,

There.

12

Main tent.

HOST I shook it off. I couldn't have done anything I haven't even digested my trail bar yet.
I follow you into the main tent and squirrel myself into a corner.
There's someone on Zoom.
Talking to someone on Zoom.
About the future of Zoom.
You're in the audience. I keep recognising people from Question Time where no one answers any questions, and Laura Kuenssberg's Bench where no one answers any questions.
They all treat you like it's your house. Everywhere you go. Still, Still after everything.
Like everything's your big fuck off house.
And when they're not with you, they act like it's theirs.
They hope one day it Will be theirs. I hope. I hope.
I hope your guests have been on holiday.
I hope when they see you, the ones you see once a year, I hope they have a lot to say.
I hope their years have been expansive. I hope that they've been fed.
I hope that they're happy, healthy and tanned.
All my guests are dead.

I hope your guests have paper hats. And argue with their nan.
I hope they diffuse the air with a naughty joke.
Forgetting what was said.
I hope they have a fag. And a fag. And a fag.
All my guests are dead.
I hope all is forgotten when the taxi comes.
I hope there's an afters in the pub, old rivals breaking bread.
I hope when the bell rings no one actually goes home.
All my guests are dead.
I hope your guests enjoy a bit of coke.
I hope that they get caught. I hope that they get caught mid-line in the toilets on the lash.
By their boss or best friend's dad.
I hope they freeze, expect the worse, careers flash before their eyes.
I hope at the last minute they are saved, by daddy producing his own stash.
I hope your guests can touch each other.
That they kiss on the lips instead.
Cheek to cheek is just for summer,
All my guests are— *(jumps out of his skin)* *—FUCK me you are So fit.*
Ruinme Please has just walked into my hiding place.

.

Hello. Did you hear that? Yeah yeah I wrote that myself. It's about Tories.

.

You look just like a paramedic I met once.

Do you fancy,

Black.

13

Instagram Live. **HOST** *is stood centre stage, looking serene.*

RUINME *(pre-recorded)* Thanks babe.

A door closes.

When **HOST** *speaks a mouthful of cum falls out of his mouth. He doesn't make any reference to it.*

HOST I feel so much better.
Zen.
So. Here we go. Phone, dash cam, get ready trolls we're going live in
3
2
1

Spotlight. An 'Instagram Live' icon flashes.

HOST Goooooood afternoon and welcome to the Mypopic Technology Showcase—an event usually shrouded in secrecy—until today.

Humbly billing itself as the Met Gala of tech networking events, the elite and super rich gather here to rub dicks and tits and play with brand-new toys and spill insider gossip that will anticipate the global tech market for, I dunno, the next ten years? Let's see what's for lunch shall we.

@mattianmishka **it's pigs in blankets time and I'm HUNGRY**

There's Inventedtheinternet Boatshoes and Dianasbalding, hovering near a buffet cooked entirely by ChatGPT. An ex-Tesla engineer clutching a half pint is holding a casual walkthrough of a new electric car that will drive from LA to San Francisco at eighty miles per hour with the aircon on full on just an hour of charge. A wagyu steak sits lonely on an abandoned plate,

@lilywins_93 **spit on it!!!**

HOST Notsuzanna sips a midday cocktail with Cokeytits Neglachef.

@mambonumber4 **icons**

HOST Trays of burgers whizz past from blonde servers on roller skates, 'Lab Grown, Try Me!'

Signposts for later talks:

The Business Smarts Behind Comic Relief

Server Plants In The City, Hiding In Plain Sight

And. There. Final Billing. You. The Pigfucker talk.

Crisis In The Name of Control, Your Business Plan Against The Grain

HOST Promising a masterclass in spin, in sleight of hand, from the cunt that got away with setting the country on fire and fucking off on holiday.

@k8remrem **BINGOOOOOOOO**

HOST My phone sings. This is where damage can really be done, let the pompous fucker destroy himself once and for all,

@len_on_the_organ **How's his lil ted talk gonna sound outside of that wank chamber!!!!!**

HOST I'll stream it all.

FRAZZLED There.

HOST I spin. Frazzled Boggler, magnificent in her power stance, her hair ringed by the sun.
Aggressively Organised behind her, an anime villain, rectangle glasses reflecting complete white.
Something hits me from behind. My phone comes loose and is thrown away from me.
Everything wobbles. My cheek is on the grass.

She's holding my unlocked phone in her hand and her face is visible on the Live for the last second.

AGGRESSIVELY *(sweetly)* That's all folks.

The live ends.

14

The staff tent.

HOST I think I've fucked it.

FRAZZLED You've absolutely fucked it.
You know your Instagram Lives are geotagged?
Thank God you asked me to mute your account to the rest of the group.
If it had got back to the front-of-house team they'd have just fired everyone. On the spot. No pay.
What are you, fourteen? You literally almost shut down the entire event for a bunch of Russian bots.

HOST *You look like a paramedic I met once.*

FRAZZLED TikTok would have been better. They'd have no idea where to look on it.
And maybe get some sleep. You look insane. And clean yourself up. Is that [cum]?

For the first time **HOST** *wipes his chin with his tee shirt.*

FRAZZLED And I'd avoid Nothingbehind Theeyes for the

rest of your life, he thinks you're the journalist assassin.
They told me to delete everything off your
phone. Everything you've been recording. All our
conversations. Creepy by the way.
A photo won't take them down. You should know that by
now. If you really wanted to kill one you'd have to knock
them out, then mummify them with gaffa tape till they
suffocate.

.

FRAZZLED I didn't delete anything by the way.
And I don't have Tory eyebrows,
Prick.

HOST She leaves.
Isn't that weird?
Frazzled Boggler doesn't have Tory eyebrows.
And that's when the jetpack takes off.

A jetpack takes off and blasts into the next scene.

15

Terrace, chaos.

HOST It starts as a speck on the horizon, then at
superhuman speed he flies across the sky,
Truly the most mental and iconic thing to happen all
day—you can buy them at your local Selfridges.

The entire crowd hypnotised by the freewheeling man
skimming a low-hanging cloud,
Then swimming into the clear open blue under the sun.
He's looping around on the field opposite, they're all
pressed against the far fence—yellow earplugs in—well
done team.
And then, I see. You. Going into the main stage. Isolated
and alone.
I don't even think and I'm sprinting across the terrace.
I grab the Gorilla Tape left unchecked in my bag. There's
a teal Chilly's water bottle left on the side by the door.
I can move fast, smash your head in. Knock you out, at
least daze you.
Tackle you to the ground, hogtie you, turn you into the
pig you once fucked, spread for all to see.
You never got away with shit. Justice always prevails,
history's greatest lesson.
Watchdog, Panorama: We All Pay In The End.
Your time to pay, and my time.
My time to do something good.

The noise peaks, then it all stops.

Act III

I'm a Star

In complete black, an audio recording of the TikTok viral 'I'm a Star' scene from Pearl. *The audio is interlaced with screams and Pearl speaking.*

'NO I'M A STAR. PLEASE I'M A STAAAAAAAAAR.'

16

The auditorium. Spotlight on Largeforehead wrapping up his intro from the prologue.

LARGEFOREHEAD Allow me to introduce our final speaker of this year's Myopic colloquy. Who navigated the country's practically teleological shift in 2016's political landscape, for better or for worse, using deft sleight of hand and masterful curation of flare-gun-suicide press exposés—Oink Oink,

Laughter.

Now please give a whopping Myopic welcome to
Our honorary gentleman,
Pigfucker, the floor is yours.

Huge round of cheering and applause.

HOST In Stephen Hawking's swan song, he wrote alongside US physicist James Hartle that when it happened, the big bang wouldn't create just one universe—but an endless supply.
I like to disappear into a grain of the chaos of this theory, that in another reality my problems have been solved, are not real or the most peaceful scenario: I do not exist.
The stage looks beautiful.
In the seven minutes it takes to subdue and hogtie an ex-prime minister, I instead taped over 346 Harlequin Lilies and their drooping willow leaves in an arch that spans from wing to wing.
Some I even manage to hang in thick twists of matte grey Gorilla Tape, cutting through the vivid colour of the flowers in such an aesthetically pleasing way it's almost an optical illusion.
Nothingbehind Theeyes and Aggressively Organised eyeball me and my impromptu decorations from the back of the audience, but they can't do anything without making a scene—they needn't be worried anymore.
I am defeated. I'm not gonna do anything drastic, violent.
I listen to the big men talk about setting up deckchairs on top of bonfires,
And hold onto the jug of water in case they need a refill.

.

Towards the end of the talk one of the lilies comes loose and falls, leaving a sunset trail of pollen that catches in the stage lights like smoking amber.
Pigfucker, remember, you even held out your hand to catch some and the audience gently crooned, as much in the palm of your hand as the gold dust I gave you.

17

Back to the barn, and straight to You.

HOST I don't suppose they notice me slip out.
The day ends perfectly, another glistening success. The warm noise of cheering and applause reaches out to me as I walk.
Maybe I should feel good, I contributed to that noise after all.
It sounds like a standing ovation. It's really fucking loud.
It's like they're cheering right behind me, like actually behind me.
It's almost like,

NOTHING WHAT DO YOU MEAN THEY'RE LILIES?

HOST I can't tune in properly. I crouch down, touch the floor.

NOTHING WHY ISN'T THE AMBULANCE HERE YET?
WHERE ARE THEY?
NO ONE TOLD ME THEY WERE LILIES THEY DON'T

LOOK LIKE,

FUCKING. LILIES.

HOST Screaming. Not cheering. Screaming.

Behind me, the main tent, the crowd dispersing and reforming around something in panic,

Flanked by thumbs in suits.

A small car? No. A table?

Quieter.

NOTHING IT'S THE FLOWERS, HE'S ALLERGIC TO THE FLOWERS.

HOST Nothing Behindtheeyes sprints past me, out the door and down the hill.

And in a surreal moment which definitely shouldn't be happening.

Something that defied all principles of responsibility, accountability and realism, but Happened.

The root of the tree where grow my problems rolling to a stop at my feet.

Gift wrapped on a teal green medical stretcher.

NOTHING THE FLOWERS... THE FLORIST.

WHERE IS THE FLORIST? THAT WOMAN. LOOKSLIKE FLORENCEPUGH.

I DON'T HAVE HER CONTACT, SHE'S NOT ON THE LIST I CAN'T SEE HER ON THE LIST

SHE'S NOT ON THE—

List.

HOST You look horrendous. A violent purple overflowing the seams of your suit, the swelling all over your body that doesn't seem to show any signs of slowing and the only ambulance route blocked by a space grey Tesla on the grass.

.

I think about apologising to you.
Or pushing you down the hill.
I imagine the bloated corpse of the man who fucked a pig secure his future tumble to his grisly end in a sty, when I shit you not,
It opens.
The broken door of the hidden cloakroom, the cloakroom that can only be opened from the inside, the invisible divide in the Silver Birch.
My invisible troll army go nuclear.
And very much like in the aftermath of a seismic blast, all songs and dust,
I do not recall the last five seconds.
I could not tell you whether you were heavy or not, whether I easily unstrapped you off the stretcher, if anyone saw me drag you over the threshold.
It is here (if you haven't already) where you must fully suspend your disbelief because in those moments, I was not conscious.
Just a chunk of hurling debris carrying you with me.

Download TikTok.

HOST As if this was always going to happen, our future mapped out in front of us.

Create a new account

HOST A prophecy we could both not be aware of or the mistakes along the way would have never fallen into place.

'@ttentionwhore'

Sorry, username taken :(please choose another.

HOST Our punishments alone and in the dark.

'@ttentionwhore2.0'

HOST Our shared, iridescent redemption hung above our heads, shining and unfurling.

Congratulations. Welcome to TikTok!

HOST In other words: Content.

Doja, SZA 'Ding'

Blackout.

EPILOGUE

Content

18

All theatricalities stop. House lights up.

PIGFUCKER *is fully clear for the first time in gruesome detail. It is obvious that he needs urgent help.*

HOST So there we are. That's everything.
It's the end now. Our story, posted.
And we're live. My first TikTok live!
You're famous, Pigfucker. Genuinely more famous than when you were in power—which don't feel weird about, it says more about the size of TikTok than it does your career.
Me running in front of you over and over on a fifteen-second loop, sandwiched in between lesbians making pasta and screaming frogs.
This is the trough you die on.
Pigfucker you are standing trial for being a cunt.
For something you initially opposed but intentionally pricked the condom and gave birth to, hoping the twisted glow of motherhood would elongate your stagnant time in office.

For everything committed by your generation of men,
generation of government.
The government past. The government now.
Do you remember the two cases of Bollinger that were
mistakenly delivered to the front of Downing Street
instead of the delivery entrance in the Spring of 2015?
Do you remember giving Boris a bus promising the NHS
350 million pounds a week?
It's almost like you foresaw what was going to happen,
some weird prophetic fearmongering.
In some very odd, very real reality, in the realm of
infinite possibility, in the theory of Hartle-Hawking's
Multiverse, your promised version of Brexit saved the
NHS from COVID-19.
May the version of you that lives in that universe live a
long and happy life.
May the version of you driving that bus be followed by
chemtrails of traffic filled with screaming fans.
May that version of you retire gracefully, with an
international display of affection, BBC dramas detailing
your life, career and fervent activism, your honest rise
to power.
May the week you die become seven days of mourning.
Let all buses across the land be redressed in the jackets
that started it all: 'LET'S FUND THE NHS INSTEAD'.
The cathedral doors remain open during the ceremony,

the casket open. Your face the peaceful mask of a man
who lived long and lived healthily.
They even name a constellation after you.
Cameron's Stethoscope.

.

This is all detailed in the ceremony. In the universe
where you didn't lie.
In that universe, the day you didn't lie becomes a
national holiday.
And in another universe, I worked a fancy event under
an old boys' club rule and told you where to shit.
And in this one my best friend died in A&E waiting for
twenty-seven hours and I think I'm still there.
My best friend died waiting for twenty-seven hours in
A&E and I think I'm still here.

.

I hope your guests can touch each other, In their
varnished wooden halls.
I hope their fuckbuddies taste like wine and cheese.
I hope they give phenomenal head.
I hope your guests expense all they cut.
I hope they build castles for all of their ducks.
And those duck houses best fucking have moats.
It's funny, the people you cut are dead.

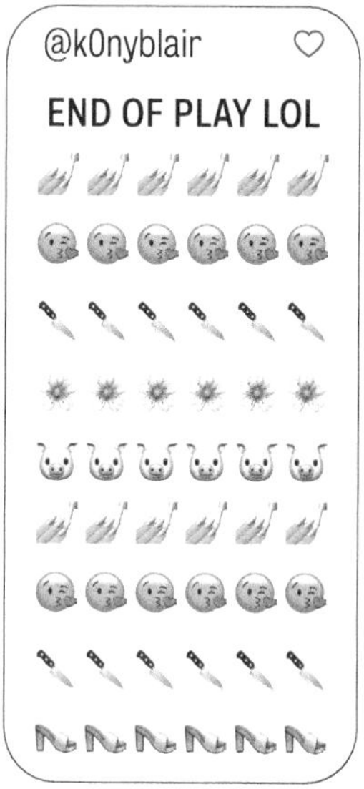
@k0nyblair
END OF PLAY LOL

Polari Press

Taking our name from the secret slang Polari, we are an independent publishing house that seeks out hidden voices and helps them be heard.

Although Polari was spoken almost exclusively by gay and bisexual men, the nature of clandestine meetings of the mid-1900s, when homosexuality was still criminalised, brought together people from all walks of life who all had an influence on the language.

Cockney, Romany, and Italian languages mixed with the colloquialisms of thespians, circus performers, wrestlers, sailors, and wider criminal communities to create a slang to express their sexuality secretly and safely.

Inspired by these origins, we publish queer voices as well as other marginalised groups, to share our perspectives with each other and help build a collaborative platform for all of us.

polari.com

Polari Plays

We are creating an active archive for queer-authored play scripts and performance.

For a complete listing of Polari Plays titles, visit:
polari.press/plays

Follow us on social media:
@PolariPress